Also by Jim Powell

IT WAS FEVER THAT MADE THE WORLD (1989)

SAPPHO

A Garland

SAPPHO

A GARLAND

The Poems and

Fragments of Sappho

Translated by Jim Powell

Farrar Straus Giroux

New York

Library of Congress catalog card number: 93-73349

ACKNOWLEDGMENTS
Grateful acknowledgments are made to the editors of *The Berkeley Poetry Review* and of *The New Republic*, and to the Reed College Small Press Collective, who published early versions of some of these translations; to the University of Chicago Press, for permission to reprint "Artfully adorned Aphrodite" from my collection of poems, *It Was Fever That Made the World*, where it appears as "Sappho: To Aphrodite"; and to the editors of *TriQuarterly*, a publication of Northwestern University, where an earlier version of "Sappho: A Garland" and much of the "Afterwords" appeared in issue 86, March 1993.

Excerpt from *Paterson* by William Carlos Williams, copyright © 1958 by William Carlos Williams. Reprinted by permission of New Directions Publishing Corp.

To Beth, to Anjanette, to Carlo, and to Joey

Contents

SAPPHO

A Garland

*Square brackets indicate gaps in the text where
the papyrus is torn or the citation breaks off.*

An asterisk indicates the end of a poem or fragment.

Artfully adorned Aphrodite, deathless
child of Zeus and weaver of wiles I beg you
please don't hurt me, don't overcome my spirit,
     goddess, with longing,

but come here, if ever at other moments
hearing these my words from afar you listened
and responded: leaving your father's house, all
     golden, you came then,

hitching up your chariot: lovely sparrows
drew you quickly over the dark earth, whirling
on fine beating wings from the heights of heaven
     down through the sky and

instantly arrived—and then O my blessed
goddess with a smile on your deathless face you
asked me what the matter was *this* time, what I
     called you for this time,

what I now most wanted to happen in my
raving heart: "Whom *this* time should I persuade to
lead you back again to her love? Who *now*, oh
     Sappho, who wrongs you?

If she flees you now, she will soon pursue you;
if she won't accept what you give, she'll give it;
if she doesn't love you, she'll love you soon now,
     even unwilling."

Come to me again, and release me from this
want past bearing. All that my heart desires to
happen—make it happen. And stand beside me,
        goddess, my ally.

        *

A *Prayer for Charáxos*

Cypris and you Nereids, bring my brother
back to me unharmed: let him sail home safely:
grant that every one of his heart's desires
        all be accomplished

once he makes amends for the present straying
of his ways, returning to bring great gladness
to his friends and ruin upon our enemies.
        No longer a worry

to his sister, let him consent to do her
honor, just this once, and her cruel sorrow [

        *

And One for His Mistress

Aphrodite, Cyprian, let her find you
at your very prickliest: don't let Dorícha
crow about him coming a second time to
        the love she is missing.

        *

Most beautiful of all the stars
O Hesperus, bringing everything
the bright dawn scattered:

you bring the sheep, you bring the goat,
you bring the child back to her mother.

*

I have a beautiful little girl: the golden flowers
are no match for her loveliness, my darling Kleïs
—for her, I wouldn't take all Lydia or sweet [

*

] for my mother said

that when she was a girl if you
bound the locks of your hair in back,
gathered there in a circlet of plaited purple,

that was truly a fine adornment,
but for blondes with hair yellower
than a torch it is better to fasten it

with fresh garlands of flowers in bloom,
and more recently there were headbands
decorated in Sardis, elaborately

embroidered [
] Ionian cities [
[   ]

But for you, dearest Kleïs, I
have no intricate headband and
nowhere that I can get one: the Mytilénean

[   ]
[   ]
[   ]

these memorials of the exile
of the children of Kléanax
  ] horribly wasted [

*

In the house of the Muses' servants
grief is not right. It would not suit us.

*

Wealth without virtue is no harmless neighbor.

*

When anger spreads inside your breast
keep watch against an idly barking tongue.

*

But I'm not one of those with a resentful
temperament: I have a quiet heart.

*

I don't expect to touch the sky with my two hands.

*

"Sweet Mother, I can't weave my web
overcome with longing for a boy
because of slender Aphrodite."

*

And you, my Dika, crown your lovely locks with garlands,
twining shoots of anise in your tender hands,

for the blessed Graces come the sooner to those adorned
with flowers, and turn away from the ungarlanded.

*

Though it isn't easy for us to rival
goddesses in the loveliness of their figures [

*

maidens [
keeping vigil all through the night till morning
used to sing the song of your love and of your
     violet-robed bride.

But wake up. March off to the young unmarried
men who shared your childhood and beg their presence
so that we may look on less sleep than does the
     clearvoiced nightingale.

*

Cretan women once danced this way
on gentle feet in time
around the lovely altar, softly
treading the tender flowers of grass.

*

O you rosy-armed Graces, hallowed Daughters of Zeus, be here!

*

whether Cyprus keeps you or Paphos or Panórmos

*

] summit of the
mountain descending,

come to me from Crete to the sacred recess
of this temple: here you will find a grove of
apple trees to charm you, and on the altars
frankincense fuming.

Here ice water babbles among the apple
branches and musk roses have overshadowed
all the ground; here down from the leaves' bright flickering
entrancement settles.

There are meadows, too, where the horses graze knee
deep in flowers, yes, and the breezes blow here
honey sweet and softer [
[   ]

Here now you, my goddess [   ] Cypris
in these golden wineglasses gracefully mix
nectar with the gladness of our festivities
and greet this libation.

*

The moon appeared in all her fullness
and so the women stood around the altar.

*

He is dying, Cytheréa, Adonis the delicate. What shall we do?
"Beat your breasts, girls, and tear your clothes."

*

] throws peace into turmoil
] weariness overcomes the heart
] settles down
] but come now, friends, dear girls,
] for day is near.

*

In Answer to Alcaeus

[   ]
"I want to tell you something, and yet my shame
    prevents me . . ." [
        [   ]

But if you wanted good things or lovely ones
and if your tongue weren't stirring up something bad
    to say then shame would never hide your
        eyes: you would state your case [

*

But stand before me, if you are my friend,
and spread the grace that's in your eyes.

*

And since you are my friend
get yourself a younger bedmate
for I can't bear to keep house together
being the elder.

*

As a poet of Lesbos surpasses foreigners

*

Let me wish the child of the house of Polýanax
a most good day.

*

Now to delight my women friends
I'll make a beautiful song of this affair.

*

Surely once you too were a delicate child:
come now, sing this, all of you, add your voices
to our celebration and grace us with your
        company [

Yes, for we are off to a wedding: you too
know this art, so hurry and send away all
the unmarried women, and may the gods [
        ] have [

For there is no pathway up great Olympos
        ] for humankind [

*

There a bowl of ambrosia
was mixed and ready
and Hermes took the pitcher and poured wine for the gods.
They all held glasses
and made libations, praying all good things
for the groom.

*

Eros arrived from heaven wrapped in a purple mantle.

*

golden chickpeas grew along the shore

*

Come to me now, you delicate Graces and you fairtressed Muses

*

Cyprus [
The herald came [
Idaíos the swift messenger
[   ]
" . . . and all the rest of Asia [   ] undying glory.
Hector and his companions escort a dartingeyed
woman from sacred Thebë and fair Plakía's streams,
delicate Andromache, aboard their ship
on the salt sea, and with her many golden bracelets
and scented purple robes and intricate adornments,
silver goblets past numbering and ivory."
So he said. His father leapt up eagerly
and word went to his friends throughout the spacious city.
The sons of Ilus led out mules and harnessed them
to fairwheeled carriages and all the crowd of women
and girls with slender ankles climbed on board [
and Priam's daughters separately [
And all the young unmarried men led out their stallions
and harnessed them to chariots, spirited [
         ] charioteers [

[*several verses missing*   ]

                              ] like the very gods
                              ] pure [
                              ] toward Ilion,
the sweetvoiced flute and cithara were mingling,
the clash of castanets, and girls' clear voices singing

a holy song. The sound rang out and reached the sky
    ] wonderfully, lau[
Everywhere through the streets [
wine bowls and cups [
and myrrh and cassia and frankincense were mingling.
The women who were older raised a joyful cry
and all the men sang out on high, a lovely song
calling on Paian, the Farshooter, skilled with the lyre,
in praise of godlike Hector and Andromache.

    *

To what shall I best liken you, dear bridegroom?
Most of all to a slender sapling I liken you.

    *

As a sweet apple reddens
on a high branch

at the tip of the topmost bough:
The apple-pickers missed it.

No, they didn't miss it:
They couldn't reach it.

    *

For you, O bridegroom, there was never another girl like this one.

    *

We will give her, her father says.

    *

Fortunate bridegroom, now the marriage that you prayed for
is accomplished, you have the girl for whom you prayed,
and *you*, bride, your appearance is full of grace, your eyes
are gentle and love wells on your delightful face:
Aphrodite has honored you beyond all others.

*

Lift high the roofbeam,
Hymenaeus,
lift high, you carpenters:
Hymenaeus,
the groom is coming, Ares' equal,
greater far than a mortal man.

*

The feet of the doorkeeper
are seven fathoms long,
his sandals are of five oxhides,
ten shoemakers worked to stitch them.

*

As a hyacinth in the mountains that men shepherding
tread underfoot, and to the ground its flower, all purple [

*

"Virginity, virginity, where have you gone and left me?"
"Never again will I come to you, never again."

*

Farewell, O bride, farewell O honored groom, farewell

*

These are Timas's ashes: on the threshold of her marriage
she died and entered Persephone's dark house instead,
and all the girls who were her friends took fresh-honed iron
to the long locks of their lovely hair and laid them on this grave.

*

Hékate, the shining gold attendant of Aphrodite

*

Come to me once more, O you Muses, leaving
golden [

*

For they say that Leda once found a hyacinth
colored egg, all covered [

*

Now Leto and Niobe were very dear companions

*

] to Phoibos the Goldenhaired whom Koios' daughter bore
                    ] to Kronos' Son of mighty name.
But Artemis made a vow and swore the gods' great oath:
"By your head, I will remain a virgin always
      ] hunting upon the peaks of lonely mountains.
      ] come, nod your head, grant me this favor."
So she said. The Father of the blessed gods consented,
and so the gods and people, too, call her Deershooter
      ] and also Virgin Huntress, a mighty title.
                    ] and Eros never approaches her [

*

The moon has set
and the Pleiades; it is the middle
of the night and the hours go by
and I lie here alone.

*

Earth with her many garlands
is embroidered

*

spring's messenger, the lovelyvoiced nightingale

*

When the pigeons' spirits grow cold they let their
wings droop at their sides. [

*

                              ] I will let my body
flow like water over the gentle cushions.

*

when nightlong slumber closes their eyes

*

O Dream on your dark wings
you come circling whenever sleep descends on me,

sweet god, and by your power
keep off the cruel memory of pain.

Then hope gets hold of me that I won't share
anything that the blessed gods [

for I would not be so [
these toys [

But may I have [
them all [

*

O beautiful, O graceful girl

*

I don't know what to do. I have two thoughts.

*

a tender girl picking flowers

*

In my season I used to weave love garlands.

*

a sweetvoiced girl

*

far more melodious than the lyre,
more golden than gold

*

over the eyes night's black slumber

*

Delicate girl, in the old days
I strayed from you, and now again [

*

Not one girl, I think, will ever look on the sunlight
of another time who has such talent as this one does.

*

Do I really still long for virginity?

*

　　] don't you remember [
we, too, did such things in our youth

*

Fool, don't try to bend a stubborn heart.

*

　　] but intricate sandals
covered up her feet, a delightful piece of
　　Lydian work.

*

mingled with colors of every kind

*

] toward you beautiful girls my thoughts
never alter

*

Come now, my holy lyre,
find your voice and speak to me.

*

I was in love with you, Attis, once, long ago.
To me you seemed a little girl, and not too graceful.

*

You have forgotten me
or else you love some other person more than me.

*

Then love shook my heart like the wind that falls on
     oaks in the mountains.

*

] You came, and I was mad to have you:
your breath cooled my heart that was burning with desire.

*

with what eyes?

*

As the stars surrounding the lovely moon will
hide away the splendor of their appearance
when in all her fullness she shines the brightest
     over the whole earth

*

Like a child to her mother I have flown to you.

*

[   ]
[   ]
           ] hope of love [
     [   ]

   ] for when I look at you face to face [
then it seems to me that not even Hermione
matched you, and comparing you with blond Helen's
     nothing unseemly,

if that is permitted to mortal women.
Know this in your heart [
        ] would free me from all my worries
     [   ]

      ] dewy banks [
[   ]
      ] all night long [
     [   ]

*

Eros the Limb-loosener shakes me again—
that sweet, bitter, impossible creature.

*

But Attis, to you the thought of me grows
hateful, and you fly off to Andromeda.

*

Why, O Írana, does Pandíon's daughter the swallow
wake me?

*

Just now Dawn in her golden sandals [

*

Never yet, O Írana, have I found
anyone more vexing than you.

*

Mistress Dawn

*

For me
neither the honey
nor the bee.

*

To Andromeda

That country girl has witched your wishes,
all dressed up in her country clothes
and she hasn't got the sense
to hitch her rags above her ankles.

*

Another to the Same

When you lie dead there will be no memory of you,
no one missing you afterward, for you have no part
in the roses of Piéria. Unnoticed in the house
of Hades, too, you'll wander, flittering after faded corpses.

*

certainly now they've had quite enough
of Gorgo.

*

And Aphrodite said
"Sappho, you and my attendant Eros" [

*

Sappho, why do you summon Aphrodite
rich in blessings? [

Andromeda certainly has her fair return.

*

Beauty is beauty only while you gaze on it,
but one who's good will soon be beautiful as well.

*

Eros, weaver of tales

*

May the winds and worries bear off the one who
blames me in my anguish [

*

                                    ] since whomever
I do well by, they are the very ones who
          injure me most of all.

*

Close beside me now as I pray appearing,
Lady Hera, gracious in all your majesty,
you whom the Atreídai invoked to help them,
          glorious princes,

while they were completing their many labors,
first at Ilion, and then on the ocean
sailing for this island: they hadn't power to
          finish their journey

till they called on you, on the god of strangers
Zeus, and on Thyóne's delightful son:
now I too entreat you, O goddess, help me
          as in the old days. [

*

Please Abánthis, your Sappho calls you:
won't you take this Lydian lyre and play
another song to Góngyla while desire still
    flutters your heart-strings

for that girl, that beautiful girl: her dress's
clinging makes you shake when you see it, and I'm
happy, for the goddess herself once blamed me,
    Our Lady of Cyprus,

for praying [

    *

May you sleep upon your gentle companion's breast.

    *

Please, my goddess, goldencrowned Aphrodite,
let this very lot fall to *me*.

    *

In my eyes he matches the gods, that man who
sits there facing you—any man whatever—
listening from closeby to the sweetness of your
    voice as you talk, the

sweetness of your laughter: yes, that—I swear it—
sets the heart to shaking inside my breast, since
once I look at you for a moment, I can't
    speak any longer,

but my tongue breaks down, and then all at once a
subtle fire races inside my skin, my

eyes can't see a thing and a whirring whistle
        thrums at my hearing,

cold sweat covers me and a trembling takes
ahold of me all over: I'm greener than the
grass is and appear to myself to be little
        short of dying.

But all must be endured, since even a poor [

                *

Góngyla [

surely some sign [
most of all [
Hermes entered, the Guide of Souls [

I said, "O my Master, [
by the blessed goddess I [
have no pleasure being above the ground:

a desire to die takes hold of me, and to see
the dew-wet lotus flowers
on the banks of Acheron."

                *

[   ]
"Honestly, I would like to die."
She was leaving me, saying goodbye, her cheeks

wet with tears, and she said to me:
"What a cruel unhappiness,
Sappho, I swear that I leave you against my will."

This is what I replied to her:
"Go, fare well, and remember me,
for you certainly know how we cared for you.

If you don't, why then, I would like
to remind you [
        ] and the beautiful times we had:

for with many a crown of roses
mixed with crocus and violets
you were garlanded while you were at my side

and with many a flower necklace
you encircled your tender throat,
plaiting blossoms together to make a wreath,

and with many perfumes [
precious, queenly [
you anointed yourself [

and on beds of soft luxury
you would satisfy all your longing
for that tender girl [

Never was there a festival
at a shrine or a temple where
we were absent [

nor a grove or a dance [

                *

I miss you and yearn after you

                *

] Sardis [
often turning her thoughts to this our island.

While she lived here beside us she honored you
like a goddess for all to see:
it delighted her most to hear you singing.

Now among all the women of Lydia
she stands out, just as once the sun's
finished setting the rosy-fingered moon

surpasses all the stars, spreading her light alike
on the salt sea and over all
the wide blossoming country meadows.

Now the dew filters down in its beauty, now
roses bloom and the tender chervil
and the flowery-scented melilot.

Often, when she goes wandering she remembers
her kind Attis, and now perhaps
her subtle heart is consumed with potent yearning.

Always her thoughts turn, longing to come where we
also think of her as her song
rises over the sea that spreads between us.

*

] places success on *your* lips,
my children, the fair gifts of the deep-robed Muses
] song-loving lyre, the clearvoiced
] but age wrinkles my skin already,
my hair has become whiter than it was black, once,
] my knees won't carry
] to dance like young fawns

] but what could I do?
] not possible to be ageless
] dawn goddess, rose-armed Eos
] ends of the earth she carried
Tithónos, her love. Nevertheless, it seized him
                  ] wife, immortal
                  ] considers
                  ] might give me.
But delicacy, that's what I love, and this love
has made of the sun's brightness and beauty my fortune.

*

  ] they have honored me with the gift of
their works

*

Goddess, I spoke with you in a dream,
Cyprus-born Aphrodite

*

"O Sappho, I love you [
the Cyprian Queen [
And yet great [
all people the sun shines on [
your glory to all lands [
and even in Acheron you [

*

I think that someone will remember us in another time.

*

Some say thronging cavalry, some say foot soldiers,
others call a fleet the most beautiful of
sights the dark earth offers, but I say it's what-
      ever you love best.

And it's easy to make this understood by
everyone, for she who surpassed all human
kind in beauty, Helen, abandoning her
      husband—that best of

men—went sailing off to the shores of Troy and
never spent a thought on her child or loving
parents: when the goddess seduced her wits and
      left her to wander,

she forgot them all, she could not remember
anything but longing, and lightly straying
aside, lost her way. But that reminds me
      now: Anactória,

she's not here, and I'd rather see her lovely
step, her sparkling glance and her face than gaze on
all the troops in Lydia in their chariots and
      glittering armor.

    *

Afterwords

Sappho of Lesbos

Sappho was a native of Lesbos, an island in the Aegean off the west coast of what is now Turkey that was settled by Aeolic Greeks during the eleventh century B.C. She was probably born in Eresos around 630 B.C., but spent most of her life in Mytilene, the most important of the island's five cities. She was the daughter of Skamandronymos and Kleïs, and was orphaned at the age of six. Her family was probably socially prominent and politically active. The eldest of her three brothers, Charaxos, was a merchant trading in Egypt, where to his sister's displeasure he became involved with an Egyptian courtesan whom Sappho calls Doricha but whose actual name may have been Rhodopis. Another brother, Larichos, poured the wine for the Mytileneans at their town hall, "an office reserved," C. M. Bowra writes, "for young men of good birth and handsome appearance." Sappho had a daughter, whom she named Kleïs after her mother; the child's father may have been one Kerkylas, a wealthy merchant from Andros—or this "information" may derive from an obscene pun in an Attic comedy, since the name can be taken to mean "Prick from the Isle of Man," as David Campbell renders it. Sappho spent time in exile in Sicily during her thirties, presumably as a result of her family's political activities, but later returned to Lesbos, where her tomb was pointed out to tourists in antiquity. Her death is probably to be dated to around 570 B.C. She is reputed to have been short, dark, and ugly. Her poems quickly became famous throughout the Greek world, revered by readers and influencing later writers—dramatists as well as lyric and choral poets and, after a time, Romans as well as Greeks. Sappho herself became a figure of fable and later of drama; we know of five comedies entitled

Sappho from the fifth and fourth centuries B.C. and in his *Heroides* Ovid has great fun with the legendary character who bore her name.*

The culture of Lesbos seems to have been flourishing for at least a century (and probably several) before Sappho's birth, and in her day its intellectual and artistic life may well have surpassed that of any other region of Greece. Sappho inherited a strong and independent poetic tradition of which she was justly proud. Though virtually nothing of Lesbian lyric poetry earlier than hers survives, we do know of two poets, Terpander of Antissa (two generations before Sappho) and Arion of Methymna (one generation before her), whose works won Lesbos a name for poetry throughout Greece, and the common elements apparent in Sappho's poems and in those of her slightly younger contemporary Alcaeus testify to this tradition's continuing vigor.

In addition to lyric, Lesbos also possessed an energetic narrative tradition of epic poetry concerning the legends of Troy, a tradition parallel with and in some measure independent of Homer's. Around three generations before Sappho, her fellow townsman Lesches of Mytilene composed the *Little Iliad*, an epic poem in four books treating events between the death of Achilles and the fall of Troy. The few surviving verses of Lesches' poem show it to have been cast in thoroughly Homeric style, measure, and Ionic dialect. On the other hand, though Sappho's extant fragments on the matter of Troy and related mythological themes reveal her familiarity with Homer, in their measure, in their language, and in her handling of their subjects they exhibit her inventive independence to much more striking effect—an evolution toward particularity which suggests the vitality of Lesbian poetic tradition in the intervening century as well as the force of her own genius.

As a woman, Sappho had the good fortune to be born into a society which allowed her talent scope to develop, a culture which was, to judge by the evidence of her poems, markedly less miso-

---

* The ancient testimonia from which these details largely derive are conveniently collected in Campbell (1982). For a translation of Ovid's poem, see Verducci 124–35. Full references to the works mentioned here and throughout can be found in the Bibliography.

gynous and gynophobic than that of many Greek cities (Athens in particular). Women seem to have taken a large role in the social and religious life of Lesbos. A number of Sappho's surviving poems and fragments represent, and perhaps figured in, the rites and festivals of several goddesses, notably Aphrodite and Hera, and some speculate that she played a quasi-formal role as an initiatrix or teacher of poetry, music, dance, and the other civilized arts to young women preparing to take their part in these social rituals and religious festivities. She also wrote epithalamia, almost certainly for performance as part of marriage ceremonies. Nevertheless, the ideology and ostensible values of Lesbian society must still have been largely aristocratic, dominance-oriented, androcratic, and somewhat militarist (one Lesbian family powerful during her lifetime, the Penthilidai, claimed descent from the Achaian generalissimo at Troy, Agamemnon). Sappho's independence of mind appears not only in her explicit rejection of such values (see "Some say thronging cavalry") but in the concern with persons and the personal evident in almost all her extant work, and the insistence with which later tradition worked to transform her into a figure of comedy suggests how threatening the culture at large found her vision. To judge by the surviving fragments of her poetry (seconded by the legends and opinion of antiquity), her passional life centered on women.

The Text of Sappho's Poems

We do not know whether or in what form Sappho might have published her poetry. More than three centuries after her death two of the great scholars of Alexandria in the third and second centuries B.C., Aristophanes of Byzantium and Aristarchus of Samothrace, collected and edited her poems in nine books arranged according to meter. The first of them (poems in the sapphic stanza) contained 1,320 verses, though others were probably shorter; nevertheless, it is apparent that originally the corpus of her poetry was fairly substantial. (By way of comparison, *Sappho: A Garland*, which translates all the surviving fragments of her work that make consecutive sense, however brief, torn, or abruptly interrupted, contains around 500 verses.) Throughout the rest of antiquity Sappho's poetry continued to attract the attention and praise of readers, poets, and scholars, and in the first century B.C. it exercised a seminal influence on the flowering of the Latin lyric. Catullus translated what is probably her best-known poem ("In my eyes") and adopted its sapphic stanza in one of his own most successful lyrics, and the example of her architectonics and psychology was crucial to Horace in his *Odes*.

But by the period of late antiquity (fifth through seventh centuries A.D.), when it became imperative for ancient literary texts to be transcribed from scrolls to books in sufficient numbers if they were to have a chance of surviving the ensuing period of social upheaval and cultural collapse, the contracting literary interests of the times and the "obscurity" of Sappho's Aeolic dialect in a world where Attic Greek had triumphed combined to bring about the eventual loss of her collected poetry. There are indications that Byzantine scholars in the tenth and eleventh centuries had access to works of Sappho now lost, but if so, these texts must have perished in the flames when the Fourth Crusade sacked Constantinople in 1204.

Until the 1890s all that survived of Sappho's poetry was one complete poem quoted by the critic Dionysius of Halicarnassus ("Artfully adorned Aphrodite"), the first seventeen verses of another cited by Longinus in *On the Sublime* ("In my eyes"), and around a hundred meager fragments, usually no more than a word or a phrase referred to in passing by various ancient grammarians, philosophers, scholars, and rhetoricians whose works' survival had been sponsored by the interest of medieval schoolmasters. Since the 1890s, however, our knowledge of Sappho's poetry has been greatly augmented by the discovery of around a hundred more fragments on papyrus (one on a potsherd) unearthed by archaeologists from the sand of Egypt. All of them are mutilated in one degree or another, many far too seriously to allow them to yield consecutive poetic sense—LP 67, for instance, a scrap of a strip of papyrus torn from the middle of a column of verse to mummify a crocodile:

]nd this overhan[
]tructive spirit [
] truly did not lik[
] and now because [
] the cause neither [
] nothing much [

But these new texts also include fragments that significantly enlarge what we know of the range of Sappho's poetry and several substantially complete poems that easily number among her best extant works. Altogether, these new fragments add immeasurably to what we possess of Sappho's poetry. If our own culture could find a way to devote one thousandth as much of its resources to sifting the sands of the Middle East as it has to steeping them in blood, it is quite possible that many more of Sappho's immortal verses might be discovered there.

In our complete ignorance regarding the conditions under which Sappho might have published her poetry, we haven't the slightest means of determining how she may have arranged her collected poems, if indeed she collected them. The major modern edition of her surviving work, that of Lobel and Page, organizes the extant fragments to re-create, in outline and insofar as is possible, the arrangement of Sappho's poetry into nine books by her Alexandrian editors. We know that "Artfully adorned Aphrodite" stood first in this edition, a placement that some contend mirrored Sappho's own, but this argument is entirely speculative, and for the rest, it is clear that the organization of the Alexandrian edition according to meter (with perhaps some attention to genre as well) reflected its editors' scholarly and formalist interests rather than the artfully precise attention to sequences of disclosure evident in Sappho's poems.

In the absence of any compelling reason to do otherwise, in *Sappho: A Garland* I have taken the opportunity to arrange Sappho's extant poetry in an integrated collage or mosaic, playing off modernist techniques of poetic sequence, fragmentary montage, and stream of consciousness to create a cumulative movement that points to the integrity of her work as the surviving fragments disclose it. Allowing the briefer fragments to create contexts for one another permits them to convey more poetic sense than they can in isolation or at random, and it also clarifies the themes that unify Sappho's poems, for all their stylistic diversity. The Sappho posterity has always remembered best is a poet of intensely personal speech, and when the Egyptian papyri proved to include poems on mythological subjects in a more traditional manner, these were at first conceived as "abnormal." But further acquaintance makes it apparent that just as Sappho's most personal poems are everywhere informed by a commanding sensitivity to the resources of her poetic tradition, so these more "public" poems share in the personal intensity of her work as a whole. They are traditional in the true sense, bringing the wisdom of the past to renewed life in the vital light of present passion.

Sappho's Measures

The surest sign of the strength and articulation of the Aeolic poetic traditions Sappho inherited sounds in her measures, and this aspect of her art has exerted a marked influence on later poetry. Aeolic metrics envisions the poetic line not as a composite entity formed by the repetition of a given number of identical "feet" but as an integrated whole. Nearly all Aeolic lyric verse forms have at least one choriamb ($-\smile\smile-$) at their cores; they differ in the ways that they begin and conclude. The measure which Sappho employed most frequently (e.g., "Artfully adorned Aphrodite") and which bears her name, the sapphic stanza, can be graphed:

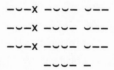

where $-$ represents a long syllable, $\smile$ a short syllable, and x an "anceps" syllable, one which may be either long or short. Ancient

Greek poetry is quantitative: it creates its rhythms by organizing the succession of longer and shorter syllables, rather than of syllables more and less stressed, as English does. By convention, the final syllable in a line may be short or long: the pause at the turn of the verse serves to fill out the length of a short syllable. Since Sappho's day a great many poets inspired by her example—from Alcaeus, Catullus, and Horace to Sidney, Campion, Hölderlin, Swinburne, and Pound—have taken up this measure, but none succeeds in matching her fluidity, ease, grace, and melodic variety. Sappho's secret consists largely in keeping her caesura moving: in her sapphics the caesura (a pause in mid-verse) seldom falls in the same place in two consecutive lines.

Another among the better-known Aeolic lyric measures is named for her poetic compatriot, the alcaic stanza (see *In Answer to Alcaeus*):

$$x-\smile-x \ -\smile\smile- \ \smile-$$
$$x-\smile-x \ -\smile\smile- \ \smile-$$
$$x-\smile-x-\smile-x$$
$$-\smile\smile-\smile\smile- \ \smile--$$

Once more the choriamb stands at the heart of the first two verses and appears in its internally compounded (doubled) form in the fourth. The logic of this complex rhythm lies in its first establishing the pattern anceps + cretic ($-\smile-$) + anceps followed by choriamb + concluding iamb ($\smile-$), then repeating it (second verse), and then repeating it again with each of its components doubled and varied: anceps + cretic + anceps + cretic + anceps followed by internally compounded choriamb + concluding bacchiac (an iamb with an additional syllable appended). Observe that if you take the initial anceps syllable of the first verse of the alcaic stanza from the beginning of the line and place it at the end, you have a sapphic verse (the form of the first three lines of the sapphic stanza above). Two more stanzaic patterns that display the logic of Aeolic rhythmic artifice with unusual clarity are the measures of "Honestly, I would like to die" and "Sardis," respectively:

```
XX  −◡◡−  ◡−
XX  −◡◡−  ◡−
XX  −◡◡−◡◡−  ◡−
```

and

```
−◡−  XX  −◡◡−  ◡−
      XX  −◡◡−  ◡−
      XX  −◡◡−  ◡−  ◡−−
```

Throughout antiquity Aeolic and Aeolic-derived measures were imitated and adapted by poets working in a wide range of genres, not only in lyrics (Theocritus, Catullus, Horace) but in choral odes (Bacchylides and Pindar) and in the choruses of Athenian drama (Aeschylus, Sophocles, Euripides). In the last two genres, where we can compare their effects with those of other rhythmic systems (Doric and Ionic) deployed in other odes or choruses by the same poets, the more intense rhythmic pleasure afforded by Aeolic measures is readily apparent.*

In *Sappho: A Garland*, I preserve Sappho's rhythms, replacing quantity with stress, wherever doing so creates a comparable effect in English. Often this means reproducing her meters exactly, though in a few places for the sake of English cadence I have admitted variations (anacrusis, feminine ending, catalexis, trisyllabic substitution) in a manner similar to her own handling of ellision, for instance. In some cases, however, Sappho's measures produce a markedly different effect in English than in Greek, and here I resort to other expedients. Translating some of the fragments that have the feel of folksong in the original, for instance, I invoke traditional English song forms, whereas to render the Aeolic dactyls of her poem on the marriage of Hector and Andromache (a meter which has an epic feel in Greek but which gallops in English) I employ a comparably epic (and unjustly maligned) English measure, iambic

* See Rosenmeyer for a lucid introduction to Aeolic metrics (and to ancient Greek metrics in general); Dale treats the development of this tradition in the choruses of Greek drama, and Page surveys the meters of Sappho and Alcaeus in an appendix.

hexameter. For the most part, though, Sappho's Aeolic measures transfer into English with remarkable felicity.

On Translating Sappho

The great British modernist poet Basil Bunting, asked what he thought of the work of one translator of Greek lyric, is said to have answered, "Oh, you mean the one who tarts up Sappho?" This is the abiding temptation which, phrase by phrase and stanza by stanza, lures translators of Sappho to a common doom, the reef upon which many a craft founders and sinks. To render Sappho's Greek literally into English is to come face-to-face with the spare, limpid, embarrassing directness of her sentences—but sentences now impoverished, disembodied, all the delightful music of her Greek stripped away and the vivid tones of her poetic voice muffled, its intense illusion of personal immediacy, of intimate speech— earnest or playful, ironic or impassioned, whispered, spoken, chanted, sung—drowned out by the dinning approximations of another tongue or replaced entirely with a language never spoken by anyone outside the classrooms of grammatical pedagogy in Greek and Latin. The first impulse of many a translator confronting such a sorry monstrosity in draft is to "make it poetic" by decorating the corpse with the ornaments approved by contemporary literary fashion. A little rouge on her cheeks, false eyelashes, a wig, and a new wardrobe in the latest style and the old girl will look good as new.

This is why most translations of poetry do not age well and why many begin to look patently preposterous after the passage of less than a generation, if they did not seem so to begin with. Fashions in poetic style, being fashions, are transitory, and once the glamorous style of a day has lost its dazzle, supplanted by the next latest mode, it no longer distracts us from the poor bare corpse it aimed to disguise. This is particularly so in Sappho's case, because often what she has to say appears, on the surface, so plain. Apart from the music of her rhythms, her intricate interweaving of the sounds of syllables, of vowels and consonants, Sappho's style seems hardly a style at all—if by poetic style we mean a characteristic manner of speaking and habits with poetic device that can be detached from what a poem has to say. This is why, though Sappho's influence shows in the works of a great many poets, hardly any have succeeded in imitating her. Her voice and her vision are consubstantial, her poetry inextricably one with the experience and the understanding it brings to speech.

Dionysius of Halicarnassus praises Sappho's combination of energy and poise in the succession of her sentences, their pace "like the onflow of a never-resting stream," and especially the smoothness with which she joins and interweaves her words to give "the effect of a single continuous utterance." This is truly and aptly observed, but Longinus comes closer to the heart of her genius when he points to the precision with which she selects and combines minutely perceived particulars of her experience, and to her detachment in observing and understanding them. Dionysius speaks of the virtues of Sappho's language, of her stylistic merits, Longinus of her attentiveness and insight, but that this attentiveness is formal as well as psychological, that for Sappho poetry is itself a mode of insight and a form of knowledge, shows in the startling variety of her poems, even as they are represented among the meager remains of her nine books: poems public and personal, amorous and consolatory, intimate, ironic, and sharp-tongued, elegiac epigram, legendary narrative, marriage songs whose tones are "popular" and "low" beside more dignified epithalamia (and still others quietly questioning the institution of marriage), hymns of religious ritual, prayers in seeming earnest and archly poetic imitations of prayers, a propemptikon and what may be a nursery rhyme . . .

Nor is this variety the result merely of a taste for generic diversity, of stylistic motives. This can be seen in the paradoxical fact that a careful, sensitive, plainly literal prose translation will convey a great deal of Sappho's intensity, as David Campbell's admirably does: so much of the power of Sappho's poetry is wrapped up in what it says. Here, though, Campbell's versions of Anacreon offer a telling term for comparison. As prose translation, they are every bit as attentively skillful as his renderings of Sappho, and yet they lose nearly everything of the Tean poet's verve and wit. Anacreon's charm (it is very like Herrick's, though much more worldly, but not as fine or as penetrating) dwells largely in the play between his sentences and the turns of his verse, whereas this interplay forms just one aspect of Sappho's art.

The virtues of Sappho's poetry do not reside exclusively in the music of her verse, any more than in her sheer rhetorical craft or generic eclecticism or deftly modulated tones of voice and turns of poetic phrasing. And yet this is what prose translations, even the best, cannot convey—not just the wit that plays between verse and statement but the pace of the verse itself, an individual poet's particular measures and ways of moving among them, their literal incarnation of a minutely particular sensibility in consubstantial terms and forms: the very body of the poem and the sense of a uniquely personal poetic presence it creates. A *Garland* adheres to Sappho's "literal sense" tenaciously, but it also aims to preserve as much as English can of the local syntactic succession of her narrative, the plot of her sentences as they unfold within and across the fall of her verses and the sequence through which they disclose her poems to the imagination, the rhythms incarnating this disclosure, and the tones of voice which at once participate in and comment on what her poems reveal. It aims, in short, to re-create the way her measures and voice embody and inform what she says. Such "merely stylistic" factors are as crucial to the local and cumulative poetic sense of her work as is its denotative content, because it is largely from them that we learn what she feels and thinks about the experience she speaks from, and a translation which failed to reflect them, or which modified them to suit the dictates of alien stylistic fashions or mores, would misrepresent her poems as surely as simple mistranslation of their "literal sense."

The melodic intensity and incandescent emotion of Sappho's poetry are often praised; her psychological penetration and irony are less widely recognized. Unlike the verbal irony of Propertius (or of most modern poetry), Sappho's is much more dramatic than linguistic—structural and situational more than verbal. It appears when we reflect on what she is telling us, and what she isn't, on the difference between what a poem says and what it implies about the one who says it. Sappho may trigger our reflections with a pointedly chosen word (the last word of "Artfully adorned Aphrodite," for example), but she prepares them in the action of her poems, in their narration. Sappho employs irony not for its own sake or to maintain a safe distance between herself and her subjects but as a means of revealing contradiction, a way of staging it. As William Carlos Williams puts it,

> Dissonance
> (if you are interested)
> leads to discovery

Sappho is interested in ironic dissonance not for the poetic frisson it produces but as a means of opening the doors of perception. Sometimes Sappho's ironies challenge the values and right-thinking assumptions of the dominant ideology of the society in which she lived, but in this she seems less intent on voicing her dissent or nonconformity from the safe distance afforded by ironic duplicity than on provoking her audience to question and reflect. And more often her ironies are directed inward. Like her poetry itself, they are a mode of insight.

Sappho's sexual nonconformity was notorious in antiquity, and it was not by assiduously aping the poetical fashions of her day that she created her poetry—a poetry so distinctive, so minutely particularized that the briefest scrap of her verses torn from the swaddlings of a mummified crocodile can with confidence be identified as hers. The reader who insists on finding a "contemporary style" in *Sappho: A Garland* will be disappointed. With some show of reason Sappho may be said to have invented the literate lyric for western literature, and as an artist she is without doubt our contemporary, but as a stylist, not remotely. Many of her poems imitate the tones of intimate, natural speech, but many others engage and play off conventions of diction and rhetoric far from conversational norms. In this they violate a fundamental assumption of most contemporary American poetry, that the proper language of poetry is natural speech, what one might in some conceivable circumstance actually say. This is a prejudice which, as a poet, reader of contemporary poetry, and creature of this time and culture, I largely share. But it is also an opinion in which, as reading in the poetry of other cultures and periods has taught me, our age is distinctly in the minority, and it seems to me that as a translator I have an obligation not to obscure this fact. In this as in other regards, to make over Sappho's verses to suit our age's taste in poetic manners—"to tart up Sappho"—would be to falsify them.

I aim instead to re-create the feel of her poetry in contemporary American English. Many recent American translations seem intent on making their originals palatable to contemporary tastes by rendering them in a generic "modern" style—poets from throughout the world and history all sounding as though they wrote only yesterday in Iowa City. Doubtless any successful poetic translation must make its original plausible and effective as contemporary verse, but to do so by making it over to suit contemporary fashion is merely to flatter transitory tastes, something enduring poetry never does. It is also to surrender much of what poetic translation—especially of ancient texts, but also of "foreign" poetry generally—has to offer both individual readers and the poetic tradition at large (besides some approximation of access to the masterworks of other cultures and ages), namely, acquaintance with other ways of experiencing and thinking about the human condition and with other ways of making poetry.

In itself such acquaintance is instructive, for it shows us that our own culture's ways of construing our lives and world are not the only ways, and so leads us to an awareness of ideology as ideology and right-thinking cant as cant. It produces a dissonance which prompts us to question the assumptions that rule our lives. Poetry is said to be essentially concerned with universal verities of human experience, verities that do not so much transcend historical circumstance and the variousness of cultures as they underlie every variety of culturally determined ideological recuperation. Beyond this encounter with other ways of thinking—once we "have got over the strangeness," learning to see through it to the human realities beyond—such acquaintance allows us to encounter what is universal in the human condition, what we share with all people in all times, and to experience it on our pulses. It offers instruction in the radical equality of all souls.

I first encountered Sappho's poems as a college freshman, in Richmond Lattimore's selection, then a few years later in Mary Barnard's complete version, and later still in Willis Barnstone's translation and one poem in Catullus's, and when I began to study Greek grammar the desire to read them in the original (even more than Homer's) was foremost among my motivations for undertaking a labor less daunting for its difficulty than for its tedium. Once I had enough Greek to do so, I got two favorites by heart and then over the next two years tried many dozens of times to translate each of them, always without success. But late one night I returned home from an especially memorable concert and, still too excited by the music to sleep, sat down once more to attempt to find a way to bring one of them into English, and by the end of the following night found that I had a draft of "Artfully adorned Aphrodite" that did not seem a hopeless travesty.

This experience taught me that Sappho would not be forced, that she would have to be approached more obliquely. Before this, and since, I have worked on translations of longer, narrative or elegiac poems, projects that seemed to yield to methodical application. But evidently Sappho's lyrics would not respond to such a coercive approach, perhaps because translating the intense gestalt of a lyric poem, like writing one, springs from a moment of clairvoyance, pressing circumstance, and luck (though it may take many nights to find the language of this moment). Certainly experience seemed to confirm this as I continued—not concertedly, and at odd moments—to work at trying to translate others of Sappho's poems. And gradually it also became apparent that I succeeded in satisfying myself with a translation, at least of one of her substantially complete poems, mostly when the issues it explores were similar to ones pressing in my own life at the time.

I go on at this length about a purely personal and strictly subjective experience because I want to register the conviction it fostered: that translations of poetry which come at all close to the spirit of their originals spring from personal affinity and from love and from luck as much as or more than from skill and knowledge and craft. This is why, I think, translations of a poet's collected works (or even of single volumes whole) are seldom uniformly successful. The reach of human sympathy and understanding is truly astonishing (far greater, I think, than most of us give it credit for most of the time), but seldom indeed will anyone, no matter how much possessed of "negative capability," be able to sympathize with every aspect of another sensibility deeply enough to speak for each one as if that very person in another language and time. If Marlowe's is still after four centuries by far the best English version of Ovid's *Amores*, this is because, when he had the genius to set himself to translating it, he brought to the process, or discovered there, aspects of himself, his life, and his poetic tradition—as a freethinker and wit, as an amorous adventurer and philosopher of love, as a poet learning and inventing his craft—deeply similar to those for which Ovid's poems speak (and one curious virtue of his translation is that Marlowe's poetry is strongest when Ovid's is strongest, and weakest when it is weakest). And here, too, is where all of us as readers enter the picture, join the dance, are woven into the garland of eternity—for here, or nowhere, in a sympathetic understanding that surpasses times and places, is the ground established where poets and translators and readers all meet,

> And for a while lye here concealed,
> To be reveal'd
> Next, at that great Platonick yeere,
> And then meet here.

I will conclude with the (to me) disconcerting reflection that the most penetrating readers of *Sappho: A Garland* will be those few who, haunted by these ghosts of Sappho's glory, find themselves driven to learn Greek in order to meet the lady herself. And so, knowing only too surely how little patience they will have with translations of ancient Greek poetry once they no longer need them,

I want to dedicate my part of *Sappho: A Garland* (since Sappho's is dedicated to all of us) to those other readers who may not find the opportunity to read her in the original and so discover the depths of my failures, and in particular to Beth, to Anjanette, to Carlo, and to Joey. If these translations were born of love and affinity, what fathered them was the desire, at different times and in different ways, that friends, and these especially, might have the chance to hear at least an echo of Sappho's voice.

Index of Sources, First Lines, and Titles

The poems and fragments are listed in alphabetical order by their opening words or title; an indication of the text I have translated follows. Variant readings and conjectures are generally from Voigt's Apparatus, but also from Lobel & Page (LP), Campbell (1982), Page (1959), and others. The number of the page on which the poem or fragment is translated appears in parentheses at the conclusion of each entry.

Editions of Sappho and Further Reading

The major twentieth-century edition of the Greek text of Sappho (together with that of her compatriot Alcaeus) is the *Poetarum Lesbiorum Fragmenta* of Lobel and Page, published in 1955.* Eva-Maria Voigt's *Sappho et Alcaeus* appeared in 1971. Its textual apparatus is considerably more extensive than Lobel and Page's, and of course somewhat more up-to-date. Though superior for scholarly purposes, however, because in the more vexed passages Voigt confines herself to reporting the evidence for the text without choosing among the possibilities, her edition is even less suited than theirs to provide a reader's text of Sappho's poetry in the original Greek. This need is admirably served by David Campbell's *Greek Lyric*, vol. 1: *Sappho and Alcaeus*, in the Loeb Library Series, which includes as well exemplary facing-page prose translations. It is the most readily available Greek text of Sappho, and the one far best suited for non-scholarly readers seeking to approach Sappho in her own language. Campbell's *Greek Lyric Poetry* contains reader's texts of most of the major poems and fragments, together with a helpful brief introduction to the peculiarities of the Aeolic dialect and notes on many difficulties of the Greek of the poems he selects. Denys Page's *Sappho and Alcaeus*, an altogether more ambitious undertaking, is invaluable for its notes on the text but often misleading in its interpretative comments (Alcaeus proves somewhat more congenial to Page's critical talents and temperament).

The best overview of Sappho in English is still probably Bowra's chapter, though his portrayal of her character reads a little quaintly today. Anne Carson explores Sappho's depiction of the psychology of desire and W. R. Johnson her manipulation of persona and strategies of address. John Winkler's chapter, "Double Consciousness in Sappho's Lyrics," considers her work partly in relation to her culture's construction of gender; it furnishes a potent antidote to centuries of scholarly prudery, misogyny, and homophobia. Merkelbach, Lanata, and Calame are enlightening regarding the likely cultic and social background of Sappho's

* For full references to the works mentioned, see the Bibliography.

poetry in the *thíasos*, *Mädchenbund*, or "women's sodality." Gentili's is the most accessible account of this discussion and offers a partial corrective to the false dichotomy which tends to plague it: that the relations and festivities characterizing Sappho's circle must have been either public and religious or personal and erotic, rather than all of these. Like most participants in this discussion, however, Gentili is sometimes inclined to read Sappho's poems in rather narrowly anthropological terms (Kirkwood addresses this problem in Merkelbach's case; his own treatment of Sappho is often sensitive, but needs to be read beside Russo's essay). Fränkel's and Davison's discussions retain interest; West's, Segal's, and Stanley's are three other recent essays I found provocative. The thesis of Bruno Snell's book misconstrues the increasing preoccupation with the individual sensibility evident in the development of Greek poetry between Homer and Theocritus as a transformation in the nature of consciousness rather than as an evolution in poetic and social forms and themes, but his observation that "Sappho visualized her sensations *sub specie iterationis*"—that is, from the vantage afforded by the spectacle of their repetition—is inexhaustible.

Bibliography

Bowra, Cecil Maurice. *Greek Lyric Poetry.* 2nd rev. ed. Oxford: Oxford University Press, 1961.

Calame, Claude. *Les choeurs de jeunes filles en Grèce archaïque.* 2 vols. Rome: Ateneo & Bizzarri, 1977.

Campbell, David A., ed., intro., and notes. *Greek Lyric Poetry: A Selection.* London: Macmillan, 1967.

Campbell, David A., ed. and trans. *Greek Lyric.* Vol. 1, *Sappho and Alcaeus,* 1982; vol. 2, *Anacreon, Anacreontea, and Choral Lyric from Olympus to Alcman,* 1988. Cambridge, Mass.: Harvard University Press (Loeb Library Series).

Carson, Anne. *Eros the Bittersweet.* Princeton: Princeton University Press, 1986.

Dale, A. M. *The Lyric Meters of Greek Drama.* Cambridge: Cambridge University Press, 1968.

Davison, John Armstrong. *From Archilochus to Pindar.* London: Macmillan, 1968.

Dionysius of Halicarnassus. *On Literary Composition.* Ed. and trans. W. Rhys Roberts. London: Macmillan, 1910.

Edmonds, J. M., ed. and trans. *Lyra Graeca.* Vol. 1. 2nd pr. London: William Heinemann, 1928.

Epigrammata Graeca. Ed. Denys Page. Oxford: Oxford University Press, 1975.

Fränkel, Hermann. *Early Greek Poetry and Philosophy.* Trans. Moses Hadas and James Willis. New York: Harcourt Brace Jovanovich, 1962.

Gentili, Bruno. *Poetry and Its Public in Ancient Greece.* Trans. A. Thomas Cole. Baltimore: Johns Hopkins University Press, 1988.

Greek Anthology. Ed. W. R. Paton. 5 vols. Cambridge, Mass.: Harvard University Press, 1916–1918.

Johnson, Walter Ralph. *The Idea of Lyric.* Berkeley: University of California Press, 1982.

Kirkwood, Gordon M. *Early Greek Monody.* Cornell Studies in Classical Philology 37. Ithaca, N.Y.: Cornell University Press, 1974.

Lanata, Giuliana. "Sul linguaggio amoroso di Saffo." *Quaderni Urbinati di Cultura Classica* 2 (1966): 63–79.

Lawler, Lillian B. "On Certain Homeric Epithets." *Philological Quarterly* 27 (1948): 80–84.

Lobel, Edgar, ed. *Oxyrhynchus Papyri* 21. 1–2, Fr. 2288. London: Egypt Exploration Society/Oxford University Press, 1951.

Lobel, Edgar, and Denys Page, eds. *Poetarum Lesbiorum Fragmenta*. Oxford: Oxford University Press, 1955.

Longinus. *On the Sublime*. Ed., intro., and notes D. A. Russell. Oxford: Oxford University Press, 1964.

———. *Longinus on Sublimity*. Trans. D. A. Russell. Oxford: Oxford University Press, 1966.

Merkelbach, Reinhold. "Sappho und ihr Kreis." *Philologus* 101 (1957): 1–29.

Page, Denys. *Sappho and Alcaeus*. Repr. with corr. Oxford: Oxford University Press, 1959.

Poetae Melici Graeci. Ed. Denys Page. Repr. with corr. Oxford: Oxford University Press, 1967.

Rosenmeyer, Thomas G., James W. Halporn, and Martin Ostwald. *The Meters of Greek and Latin Poetry*. New York: Bobbs-Merrill, 1963.

Russo, Joseph. "Reading the Greek Lyric Poets (Monodists)." *Arion* n.s. 1, no. 4 (1973–1974): 707–30.

Sappho. Selections, trans. Richmond Lattimore, in *Greek Lyrics*. 2nd ed., Chicago: University of Chicago Press, 1960.

———. *Sappho*. Trans. Mary Barnard. Berkeley: University of California Press, 1958.

———. Trans. Willis Barnstone, in *Greek Lyric Poetry*. New York: Schocken Books, 1972.

Segal, Charles. "Eros and Incantation: Sappho and Oral Poetry." *Arethusa* 7, no. 2 (1974): 139–60.

Snell, Bruno. *The Discovery of the Mind*. Trans. Thomas G. Rosenmeyer. Cambridge, Mass.: Harvard University Press, 1953.

Stanley, Keith. "The Rôle of Aphrodite in Sappho Fr. 1." *Greek, Roman and Byzantine Studies* 17 (1976): 305–21.

Verducci, Florence. *Ovid's Toyshop of the Heart*. Princeton: Princeton University Press, 1985.

Voigt, Eva-Maria, ed. *Sappho et Alcaeus: Fragmenta*. Amsterdam: Athenaeum, 1971.
West, Martin Litchfield. "Burning Sappho." *Maia* 22 (1970): 307–30.
Winkler, John J. *The Constraints of Desire*. New York: Routledge, 1990.

Glossary of Persons and Places

Disyllables are always accented on the first syllable.
In transliterating names I have preferred familiar forms to consistency.

Abanthis   A woman friend of Sappho

Acheron   One of the rivers of the underworld

Alcaeus   Another famous Lesbian lyric poet, Sappho's slightly younger contemporary

Anactoria   A woman friend of Sappho

Andromache   Wife of Hector (see Homer's *Iliad*)

Andromeda   An acquaintance and rival of Sappho

Atreidai   The sons of Atreus, Agamemnon and Menelaos (see Homer's *Iliad*)

Attis   A woman friend of Sappho

Charaxos   Sappho's eldest brother

Cyprian   An epithet of Aphrodite, alluding to her birth from the sea near Cyprus

Cypris   An epithet of Aphrodite, alluding to her birth from the sea near Cyprus

Cytherea   An epithet of Aphrodite, alluding to her birth from the sea near the island of Cythera (according to another story)

Dika   A woman friend of Sappho

Doricha   The Egyptian mistress of Sappho's brother Charaxos

Gongyla   A woman friend of Sappho

Gorgo   An acquaintance and rival of Sappho

Hector   Son of King Priam of Troy, the leading warrior of the Trojans in the Trojan War; slain by Achilles (see Homer's *Iliad*)

Helen   Of Troy, wife of Atreus' son Menelaos; her elopement with Priam's son Paris precipitated the Trojan War (see Homer's *Iliad*)

Hermione   The daughter of Helen of Troy; her beauty, like her mother's, was proverbial

Hesperus   The Evening Star: the planet Venus

Hymenaeus   A traditional cry of refrain in wedding songs

Idaios	A Trojan herald (see Homer's *Iliad*)
Ilion	Troy
Ilus	Eponymous founder of Ilion; the "sons of Ilus" are the Trojans
Ionia	Collectively, the Greek cities and settlements south of Lesbos on the islands off the west coast of what is now Turkey and on the mainland; in Sappho's time its culture was characterized by intellectual ferment, opulence, and refinement
Irana	A woman friend of Sappho; her name is more properly transliterated Eirana
Kleanax	Patriarch of a powerful family on Lesbos, father of the tyrant Myrsilos
Kleis	Sappho's daughter
Koios	Father of Leto
Kronos	Father of Zeus
Leda	Mother of Helen of Troy and of Castor, Pollux, and Clytemnestra
Lesbos	Sappho's home, an island off the northern west coast of what is now Turkey, settled by Greeks in the eleventh century B.C.
Leto	Mother of Apollo and Artemis
Lydia	An Asiatic kingdom on the southwest Turkish mainland, proverbial for opulence and luxury
Mytilene	The most important of the five cities of Lesbos and Sappho's home
Nereids	Sea nymphs, daughters of Nereus, the Old Man of the Sea
Niobe	Sister of Pelops and wife of Amphion; she bore him seven sons and seven daughters who were slain by Apollo and Artemis after she boasted that she had fourteen children while Leto had only two (see Ovid's *Metamorphoses*)
Paian	An epithet of Apollo
Pandion	Legendary king of Athens; his daughter Philomela was transformed into a nightingale and his daughter Procne into a swallow in sanguinary circumstances (see Ovid's *Metamorphoses*)
Panormos	Probably modern Palermo in Sicily
Paphos	A city in Cyprus, one of Aphrodite's cult centers
Phoibos	Another name of Apollo
Pieria	A region of Macedonia whose Mount Pieros was sacred to the Muses; "the roses of Pieria" are the flowers of the Muses
Plakia	River near Thebe, Andromache's hometown

Polyanax	Patriarch of a Lesbian family, probably politically powerful; Sappho does not seem to have been on good terms with them
Priam	King of Troy, father of Hector (see Homer's *Iliad*)
Sardis	The capital of Lydia, proverbial for opulence, luxury, and refinement
Thebe	Andromache's hometown, down the coast from Troy
Thyone	Another name of Semele, the mother of Dionysos
Timas	A young woman, probably a member of Sappho's circle of younger friends
Tithonos	Lover of the dawn goddess Eos; she procured him immortality but forgot to request eternal youth for him as well

PA
4408
E5
P69
1993

Sappho.

Sappho, a garland.

$15.00

DATE